Khumásiyát:
poems from the moroccan desert

poems by

yahya frederickson

Finishing Line Press
Georgetown, Kentucky

Khumásiyát:

poems from the moroccan desert

ACKNOWLEDGMENTS

For inspiring the poems in this collection, I would like to thank
Cynthia J. Becker's *Amazigh Arts in Morocco: Women Shaping Berber Identity*
(University of Texas Press, 2006).

My deepest respect to the Ait Khabbash, and all Imazighen.

Thanks to Karen, Youssef, and Khadija of Café Tissardmine; Mohamed Bou
Youssef, Ali, Hassan, Christine, Heather, Khadija, Taehoon; and Dr. Michael
Beard.

And, as always, thanks to Fathia.

Publisher: Leah Huete de Maines
Editor: Christen Kincaid
Cover Art: Lindsey H. Nelsen
Author Photo: Yahya Frederickson
Cover Design: Elizabeth Maines McCleavy

Order online: www.finishinglinepress.com
also available on amazon.com

Author inquiries and mail orders:
Finishing Line Press
PO Box 1626
Georgetown, Kentucky 40324
USA

AUTHOR'S NOTE

Khumásiyát: an Arabic word derived from the three-letter root *kha-meem-seen*, meaning "five," specifically five-lined stanzas, or quintains. I've taken the liberty of expanding the meaning to include lines containing five key words each—a number that allowed a changing interplay of imagery.

In 2023, I traveled to Tissardmine, a village in the desert of southeastern Morocco, to be a writer-in-residence at Café Tissardmine, a space for artists. It was my first time in the Moroccan Sahara. I had brought many drafts of work in various stages to occupy my time, but the place—as places often do—pulled me to respond.

Each day, I took a long walk in a different direction. Despite many people's assumptions, the Sahara is not endless sand dunes. Actually, most of it is *hamada* (a hard, baked plain), with rocky outcroppings, dry riverbeds, oases, and yes, sand. Morocco's largest dune complex, Erg Chebbi, towers in the distance. Here, beauty is stark—wind-polished stones pushed across the plain. An acacia tree on the horizon—is it farther than it appears, or nearer? Crosshatches in the sand—the tracks of a nocturnal insect, reptile, or rodent—their terminus a small hole. A limestone outcropping that, upon closer examination, holds layers of fossilized sea life—400 million years old, the paleontologists say. Stars so three-dimensional they seem to dangle from the sky like grape clusters, unobscured by light pollution.

Another inspiration was Cynthia J. Becker's *Amazigh Arts in Morocco: Women Shaping Berber Identity* (University of Texas Press, 2006), an ethnography of the women of the Ait Khabbash, the Amazigh (or "Berber") group indigenous to the region. Especially insightful were the explanations of their textile arts, dressing, dance, and songs. Becker's research introduced me to the lives of the people with whom I interacted.

In my journal, I began listing things I saw: *star, sky, stone, palm, bird, donkey*. In Becker's book I noticed them too, as well as other things repeating in the people's textile arts, songs, and lifeways: *silver, red, heart, eye, bride, mother*.

I collected 125 words—words signifying elements of the natural world, human relations, Ait Khabbash culture, and the palette of predominant colors. I wrote each word on a slip of paper and kept the slips in a covered basket.

Then, I began my composition process. After shaking the basket, I drew out slips one by one, every five words comprising a line. I wanted to employ the randomness, let the words interact in different ways, change their parts of speech. I allowed myself the addition of plurals, articles, prepositions, and conjunctions to normalize the phrasing. These steps I repeated until all 125 slips were drawn—a poem 25 lines long.

For each new poem, I repeated the ritual. For variation, sometimes I began every line with a particular conjunction to harness the windlike energy of anaphora.

This collection does not come without potential hazards: some readers might think it an act of cultural appropriation or neo-colonialism. True, I am neither Amazigh, Moroccan, nor Arab. As a Muslim visitor I was welcomed into the small local mosque, and I conversed with people everywhere as best I could with my intermediate Arabic and the few words of Tamazight I'd learned. I try to remain conscious of my inherent privilege and the power relationship it assembles around me; I try to conduct myself as a humble, sensitive witness. If these poems do anything, I hope they reflect my gratitude, appreciation, and honor for the people who call the Moroccan Sahara home.

Yellow   eye   tears   braid   home

    sheep   sand   coin   red   fox

salt   mountain   children   sing   sun

    cord   loom   milk   sky   stone

mirror   tail   pray   green   year

    mother   egg   seven   goat   bangs

copper   sleep   stars   roam   wood

    father   *jnoun*   camel   day   arrow

feet   dust   gold   bread   meat

    silver   throat   hand   indigo   dance

almond   horse   beauty   omen   dates

    river   black   leaves   white   bag

saffron   donkey   dagger   riddle   hang

    oasis   triangle   water   horn   wool

praise   thorn   bead   heal   turban

    tomb   belt   daughter   mouth   amber

luck   morning   head   face   word

    Allah   diamond   help   dung   beetle

tent   carpet   tree   drum   heart

    palm   thread   silk   gazelle   fire

life   pigeon   skin   henna   door

    brother   knee   bride   bird   promise

cat   liver   shell   grass   flower

    wheat   blood   cockroach   shoe   night

saddle   dry   hair   moon   rain

Hand loom

      goat palms

           children

indigo bread

      silken bangs

           sheep

      black rain

           green feet

             a head

      a bride's riddle

           a triangular star

             a donkey

      seven woods

           a father's henna

             meat

turban-words

        life-water

                hair

home blood

          roaming saddle

                    grass

      oasis drums

           amber carpets

                      hanging

        a daughter's thread

           a brother's gazelle

                    sleep

       a golden tomb

            a fire heart

                   a mouth

a silver tail

　　　white almonds

　　　　　Allah

morning eyes

　　　a tree of day

　　　　　a cat

sand-dung

　　　beautiful arrows

　　　　　a liver

a mother's egg

　　　a diamond belt

　　　　　flowers

a healing year

　　　a singing cord

　　　　　beetles

a promise at night

        salt dance

                braids

red cockroach

          sky mirror

                  leaves

woolen sun

             wheat pigeon

                    saffron

a face's horn

             shoes near a tent

                      dates

moon in the throat

                copper bird

                      a knee

camel skin

        a *jnoun*'s omen

                        mountains

    a dry dagger

        stones   shells

                  coins

      a beaded bag

          the luck of milk

                       horses

      a yellow door

           a river's help

                  prayers

        dusty praise

           thorn tears

                a fox

Beauty	a father's riddle	a year of faces
fire	healing copper	a donkey's mouth
wool	milk loom	knees on carpet
brothers	a henna triangle	gazelle blood
the sky	a roaming braid	bread from the sun
night	a head in the mirror	dry dates
silver	a silky cat	the life of sand
white	starry rain	the sleep of shells
meat	wooden coins	the palm of a hand
dung	mountain thorns	a golden tail
morning	the promise of a river	the help of a beetle
water	the heart of an egg	the throat of a fox
oasis	an indigo belt	a mother's horn
horses	a hanging door	pigeons homing
dance	moon-daughter	stone luck
feet	black cockroach	singing leaves
arrows	banging drums	bird-bride
tents	a bag of prayers	seven omens
goats	children's shoes	green almonds
sheep	words for trees	a red camel
jnoun	saffron hair	yellow diamonds
flowers	a day of liver	wheat grass
a saddle	amber tears	a thread of salt
a cord	the eye of a turban	praise for a tomb
Allah	dusty beads	a dagger against skin

Shells   beads   seven almonds   a dance

a tail in water   arrows   a skin tent

goats   Allah beautifies the fox

donkey dung   silk triangles   a dagger

a looming eye   a grassy tomb   dust

a copper saddle roaming praise   cords

horns   pigeons   bangs   a day in flowers

a diamond in saffron   yellow-haired *jnoun*

the knees of sheep   green prayers   a word

an amber shoe five bags   a foot

a salt drum   a river   leaving life

the bride of a cockroach   silver   gold a door

thorns   stones songs   hanging in the throat

oasis home   a wooly white horse

the belt of a gazelle   a bird's egg in the palm

milk with blood   beetles   the promise of trees

mountains of sand   camels   the tears of children

a cat on the carpet   a brother   a handful of dates

rain on wood   lucky stars   indigo

a braided daughter   a heart   the moon   sleep

bread in the mirror   heads   the black night

a healing face   help   the reddening sky

an omen of wheat   henna   threaded liver

morning   a mother with coins   a mouth with meat

a dry father   the sun   a year of riddles

Skin of wheat, beauty of water and pigeons
white praise, triangles of bread and henna
the healing silk of a face, the tears of feet
in the oasis: a bird, a horn dagger, a drum
in the head: copper and diamonds, meat and almonds
a red sky helping the donkey father
the luck of indigo eyes and black mouths
mothers of cats, green arrows of palm
tails singing of mountain milk and saddles
prayers and riddles, the golden door of words
beetles the omens, thorns in the loom and shoes
a brother's saffron hand leaving a coin
a wooden shell, a gazelle dancing in the dust
Allah threading seven years through a heart
in the mirror, hair braided with beads and flowers
silver sleep kneeling in grass by the river
the children home, a dry cord on the fire
life: moons of salt, dates, wool
a bag of sun, a belt of roaming goats
a cockroach in the blood, a tomb of amber and dung
a starry tent on stones, the promise of an egg
a morning: foxy daughter of the day's *jnoun*
the yellow-and-liver carpet, the hanging bangs
of a camel in the throat of a bride, a sand turban
in the night rain, under a tree: horses and sheep

A face is a shell, a goat, a gazelle, a thorn
the day a daughter leaves, the door becomes a mirror
children stone a golden camel: blood
a grass bag dances in a triangular mouth
green cats, almond-arrowed sheep
a bride looms horses and indigo cockroaches
Allah's word: a year of red eggs
the night outfoxes daggers and wooden saddles
beauty: yellow dust on a white horn
the eye in the sky heals head to shoe
home: a dung fire, a hand on the tomb
coins in a prayer tent, amber in a mountain
silky luck, bread and water for *jnoun*
a milk pigeon roams for turban diamonds
silver dates and henna tears hang
from threads on seven palms during the liver moon
on a saffron morning, beads of wheat and sand
a mother bird riddles the oasis and the river
a copper braid sings to a brother's cord
a rain of stars bangs salt into a father
an omen of donkey knees and woolen flowers
the carpet promises, the drum praises the tree
there is hair. there is meat: skin, heart, feet
a belt of black tails helps against beetles
life sleeps in the dry throat of the sun

The life of a loom: dates, eggs, heads
Allah's golden day: gazelles, goats
promises left by a mirror, a bag, a dagger
a bride's tears: saffron, diamonds, arrows
the cords of night: green and black bangs
thorns around the tomb, the beauty of water in the mouth
the luck of a mountain; dancing at the door of home
a beetle roams the belt of fire for meat
dry words in the throats of carpets and henna
the healing palm sings to the silky fox
turbans, wheat, and salt above seven knees
a thread with birds hanging from a daughter's saddle
help from moon grass and sun coins
white of sky, tent, heart, and milk
in the river of dust, children with silver triangles
a horn of bread, an omen of copper and sleep
in the oasis, a skinned hand, stars like cockroaches
in the morning, father's braid with shells and dung
jnoun with tree brothers, almond mothers
red wood praises indigo sand
prayers against facial hair and pigeon blood
shoes of camel wool on liver feet
a year of riddles from the tails of amber cats
eye stones, donkey beads, drums
 sheep, horses, yellow flowers in the rain

Where are the milky tears of feet, arrows, and saddles?
where are the word-cockroaches in the silver blood of the head?
when will the cord bag do its red-tailed dance?
why are threads and eggshells in the throat of morning?
when are the years of seven mountains, of gazelle knees?
where are the white-bread stars and woolen hands?
who will praise the days of henna, wood, and copper?
whose coins bang against the liver sky above the oasis?
whose riddles hang like beads from children and horses?
whose sheep mirror prayers on almond carpets?
where do the faces of *jnoun* loom over the river like an omen?
who dusts triangles of skinned meat with saffron?
why do green-horned birds sleep above camels?
does Allah's promise roam over water and sand?
whose shoes drum, whose eyes flower to life?
why does the fox leave salt on moonstones?
why do braids of wheat sing in the father's tent?
where is home for a yellow and indigo palm belt?
where is the tomb with a golden dagger and a beautiful tree?
whose daughter has an amber cat that mouths diamonds?
whose mother is a lucky thorn, whose a dung turban?
which night helps the bride blacken the sun?
whose dates rain in the hearts of donkeys and pigeons?
how many hairs of grass beetles heal a brother?
how many silky goats? how many dry doors are on fire?

I am salt in the eyes of sheep, horses, and gazelles
I am the heart, the knees of a beetle dancing in the rain
I am a mirror, a drum, a door hanging from a palm
I am a *jnoun*'s horn, a red tail in a tree
I am asleep with daggers and arrows in the henna dust
I am at home with egg whites, stars, and stones
I am grass in the throats of goats. I am coins in the sun
I am a tomb of cat hair and healing milk
I am a bag of leaves under the face of a roaming donkey
I am a year of praising beads of mountain wheat
I am a daughter's turban firing dung and wood
I am a green diamond in a belt of silver and amber
I am the mouth of a woolen shoe helping against thorns
I am the sky flowering with shells and copper words
I am a mother's lucky cockroach on a silk thread
I am a father singing of meat and golden bread
I am a black camel triangulating the indigo dates
I am a fox's promise to a pigeon on a sand carpet
I am days of dry mornings, nights of water
I am a hand braiding birds, praying for a river
I am Allah's riddle in the head and liver of a bride
I am an almond moon looming over a saffron oasis
I am an omen of blood, seven children in a tent
I am the beauty of skin under yellow bangs and tears
I am the life of a brother's feet on a cord saddle

You are coins of blood dried black on the tomb
you are the beauty beneath a saffron tent beneath a tree beneath the sun
you are a yellow cat eating meat at the door of home
you are a year of omens, henna on donkeys and pigeons
you are Allah's words in the eyes, skin, and heart
you are a beetle sleeping on the mirror of a mother's life
you are a face of indigo wood and liver grass
you are the lucky arrow through a *jnoun*'s watery egg
you are the knee of bread a goat roams around the fire for
you are the riddle of the day, a hand with almonds and amber
you are the stones on a daughter's belt, under a brother's feet
you are the sky threading the heads of children with cockroaches
you are gazelle wool dancing through mountain flowers
you are a bride with horsehair and shells, drumming
you are helping a palm cord from a fox's mouth
you are a shoe saddled with dates, leaves, and thorns
you are the promise of bangs, a bag of moon diamonds
you are a triangle of birds on a camel over salty sand
you are a red-and-white turban healing the night
you are the silky river of a father's tears in wheat
you are green praise braided with stars and dung
you are a dusty horn praying for beads of rain
you are the tail of morning looming over a golden carpet
you are a copper dagger hanging in an oasis of milk
you are seven throats singing of silver sheep

Because the *jnoun* dance in belts and turbans of fox

because even hairy tails, dung, and fire are from Allah

because of carpet threads and donkey shoes in the sun

because a brother promises to help against horns and words

because of the daggers on indigo flowers, a river of beetles

because of a triangular liver face atop a green mountain

because water yellows in the sandy mouth of a tree

because silk, wool, and thorns are life for pigeons

because braided bread, salt, and a bird are in the mirror

because an arrowhead leaves a hand to roam

because the golden cords around camels and gazelles are lucky

because of milk and meat at the bride's feet all night

because the tomb prays on its knees for a year of mornings

because home looms over wheat and white shells

because the tears of seven children and horses are an omen

because a father coins the day's amber heart

because of the mother's palm on the almond-and-silver door

because the catty stars sing diamonds and rain

because of a grass saddle with dates, henna, and saffron

because the dry beads of eyes and eggs sleep

because a red drum heals stony skin

because of wood dust in a bag in a tent in an oasis

because of a beautiful black moon riddled with copper

because of cockroaches and the bloodied throats of sheep and goats

because a daughter's hanging bangs praise the sky

So the copper-throated fox can braid the day
so a hennaed face can promise yellow words
so dates in the hand are beads on the loom of Allah
so morning bangs pigeons against bird-tombs
so stones and cat dung roam over the carpet
so life's riddle is a head on mountain grass
so seven diamonds help a mouth sing
so a dry omen praises the green sky
so a lucky donkey leaves saffron and silver
so a black bag dusts off palm shoes
so the moon waters the feet and knees of *jnoun*
so a fiery dagger skins the door of stars
so red tears egg the night home
so a bride's threads hang from wood in the oasis
so the thorny sun has liver and triangular almonds
so the father is a beetle, the daughter a gazelle's eye
so the river's mirror mothers a year of wheat
so the cockroaches' dance in the tent heals the sheep
so there's bread, milk, wool, and meat during sleep
so the white cord is brother to the salt arrow
so there's indigo hair under the tail of a sand turban
so amber flowers rain from saddle horns
so children pray for horses, goats, and shells
so trees are beautifully belted with silk and coins
so blood drums in the golden hearts of camels

If my eyes dance from wooly bangs to a throat
if my saddle is beaded with the day's diamonds and shells
if my children leave milk near the knee-loom
if my daughter's turban is sky, amber, and indigo
if the fox heads to my fire of thorns and almonds
if the sun braids shoes for my horses and donkeys
if a riddle reddens my gold-and-copper dagger
if home eggs the face in my hand mirror
if a triangle of stars hangs omen-like over my father
if a cat roams my goat-skin tent
if saffron coins cockroaches, and salt, words
if luck is a beautiful bag of silver hair
if at the foot of a dry tree are my brother's horns
if palms in the morning are Allah's belted door
if camel hearts can pray, sleep, and heal
if meat and dates mean a night of silk carpets
if it's a year of arrows, black cords, and beetles
if a moon bird lives in henna grass
if there's a yellow river of rain over my mother's tomb
if gazelles promise praise, and sheep, dust
if pigeons stone the bride with their tears of sand
if seven *jnoun* mouth bread in the oasis
if livers bloody the water, the wheat, and the flowers
if a white tail sings for help in the woods
if the mountains drum dung into green threads

Or the help of pigeons' amber beads of praise
or a father eyeing stones in the grass like words
or a wooden heart banging against a liver sky
or a dance of blood, milk, water, and silver
or a daughter, a goat, and a gazelle hanging over a river
or a loom, on it a donkey, an arrow, a white shell
or birds on a hand-braided thread belt
or a mother's fire and her children's rain on the skin
or drums and horns on a morning of foxes and flowers
or a year saddled with the promise of cockroach heads
or the healing black night of a dusty brother
or the life of a dagger becoming meat, wheat, and saffron
or *jnoun* singing of eggs, cats, and salt
or a red-hennaed camel on a diamond mountain
or dry riddles on golden tent carpets
or the yellow coins of sun at Allah's feet
or the beauty of green dates to a sandy throat
or a triangular beetle leaving horsehair
or a copper tree sleeping in indigo silk
or a lucky home in a tomb of star tails
or bread and sheep in the bride's mouth at the oasis
or the omen of a turban with a wool cord, roaming
or a thorn in a shoe facing a mirrored door
or knees praying for seven days among palms
or a bag of dung under the moon's almond tears

Then an arrow will praise bread within an indigo tent

then a horn will drum water from a hanging carpet

then the green wooden coins of *jnoun* will become night

then a white bag will become a year of life at home

then a bride with a gazelle on a cord will be a lucky morning

then words will bang on shells for the promise of meat

then a wooly triangular face will help with sleep

then a saffron beetle in the sky will be a brother's heart

then there'll be a sand cat, a horsetail, a cockroach

then an amber turban will head to a yellowing oasis

then the silver sun will silken the hair of goats

then stony leaves will heal stars and diamonds

then the moon will loom threads of sleep into a belt

then almond flowers will pray for golden salt

then a knee will be on a mirrored saddle with birds and flowers

then Allah will blacken a daughter's tearful trees

then a beautiful hennaed throat will roam for rain

then a father's beads of blood will become fiery wheat

then there'll be seven dry thorns in palms and feet

then the door of a tomb will sing for eggs and liver

then the omen of a hand will milk a dusty donkey

then the day will riddle camels mouthing a river

then shoes with dung, daggers, and braided dates

then a mother's eye will dance over a red mountain

then over pigeon grass and the copper skin of her children

And a braid of sunlight roaming over amber dates
and a turban of silver drumming in the hennaed night
and a copper arrow in the knee of a rainy day
and coins on cords over a face praising foxes
and the blood of a beautiful, silky donkey on the mirror
and beetles in the sand and grass before a *jnoun*'s door
and a mother looming words inside white triangles
and the tears of children in the wheat firing at a heart
and the help of a camel threaded into a father's belt
and the bangs of the sky and the shod feet of the river
and the singing tombs of goat tails and dung
and blackbirds and yellow pigeons homing
and the luck of hands praying for bread and liver
and a green bag over the horn of a golden sheep
and a cat's lives and a wooden-egg moon
and milk and thorns on a daughter's sleeping skin
and an omen of flowers in the eyes, mouth, and hair
and the riddle of the horse and the indigo diamond dagger
and seven healing stones from the mountain of Allah
and a cockroach on the salty throat of a wool saddle
and almond leaves on a bride's carpet in the morning
and beads of meat beneath the trees in a brother's oasis
and saffron dust hanging in the gazelle tent
and the yearly dance of dry red stars
and the promise of handfuls of water and shells to a head

Except for an omen of goat thread and wheat on a tomb
except for a cockroach on a dried liver in the bangs of grass
except for the almond trees, eggs, and tears on a carpet
except for a diamond praising the skin's dusty coinage
except for the riddle of the mirrored drum and the black dates
except for the luck of a shell mouth and a wooden foot
except for a mother and children hanging a gazelle outside a tent
except for a knee looming over the indigo milk of a fox
except for a thorny daughter roaming for saffron pigeons
except for a cat near handfuls of braided greenery and flowers
except for a *jnoun*'s arrows singing the morning to sleep
except for the hennaed word on the door of a donkey's home
except for the oasis helping whiten a brother's hair
except for life's eyes, faces, hearts, and tails
except for a silken shoe praying over a throaty mountain
except for a father sleeping with an amber dagger in the rain
except for the yearly bag of water from the moon and stars
except for the beauty of Allah in wool and in dung beetles
except for the brick of bread promised nightly by the river
except for yellow leaves dancing in the salty sky
except for turbans, belts, and beads of horn on the sand
except for bloodstones and firebirds that heal
except for the day's golden triangles of horses and camels
except for seven corded saddles heading toward the sun
except for red meat on copper and silver among the palms

Beyond the promise of beaded skies roaming through grass

beyond the prayers of feet and eyes for diamonds and leaves

beyond the salty yellow water in a father's horn

beyond the amber-haired cat mirroring an arrow

beyond the fire helping blacken the moon's carpet

beyond the tails under sand and the dung under indigo trees

beyond the daggers, henna, and woolen belts from the mountains

beyond the cockroach, the donkey's knee, the almond doorway

beyond the morning of palms at the mouth of a motherly river

beyond the stone tears of beetles in the heart of the oasis

beyond the thorny daughter dancing triangles in wheat

beyond the dry riddles about shells, luck, and home

beyond the bread of life inside the beautiful bag of a face

beyond the omen of seven dates on a starry tomb

beyond the hand drumming for coins, eggs, and goats

beyond the saffron bride praising the healthy pigeons

beyond the years of turbans—milk, gold, blood

beyond the horse meat hanging from a brother's braid

beyond the liver in the throats of wooden children under the sun

beyond the words inside a white sheepskin tent

beyond the threads in the shoes, saddles, and heads of *jnoun*

beyond the bangs of a fox in the green rain of night

beyond the silver bird's dusty day of sleep

beyond the copper gazelle looming over the red flowers

beyond the camel's cord singing its silk to Allah

Into a sleepy turban, the words of sheep and birds
into grass, life singing with cockroaches and beetles
into the oasis, seven camels hanging by their throats
into tears, the omen of a salty cord around a tree
into the yellow carpet, a prayer for indigo dust
into the hand, an almond flower, a cat, a dagger
into a dry daughter, the watery heart of a gazelle
into a horn, the knees and feet of a saffron horse
into skin, the rainy morning sky of home
into the door of a year, Allah's beautiful coins
into a headstone, the help of wheat and sun
into the river of milk, arrows, saddles, and tents
into the mountain, silver bangs and a triangular tail
into a mother's palm, praise for eggs and thorns
into a brother's dates, beads of goat dung
into a threadbare bag, the promise of pigeon blood
into the mouth of night, a green hennaed shoe
into the children, bread and drums, looms and belts
into the liver, golden sand and black braids
into the tomb, shells, wood, and healing copper
into the eye, the white roaming riddles of *jnoun*
into the fire, a father's face of wooly hair
into the fox, donkey meat and diamond leaves
into the mirror, days of silk and lucky stars
into the moon, a bride in red and amber, dancing

Out of the omen of white camels and shells near water

out of the green tent, feet—eggs and bread

out of the stars and thorn birds hennaed onto palms

out of the door, a brother and father helping cockroaches

out of healing and roaming, a life riddled with pigeons

out of a face praying on a carpet, some sheep and a fox

out of the indigo-and-yellow fire, the donkey's daughter

out of a saddled gazelle heading for tree leaves

out of triangular bangs hanging with blood

out of the mouth of morning, promises of copper and amber

out of a bride's year at home, a black drum

out of words, grassy hair and golden braids

out of beautiful coins of meat, mountain cats

out of the rain's praise for arrows, mirrors, and dung

out of the hand, a wooden goat, a dusty shoe

out of a horn, a river of sand beneath a moonlit sky

out of the salty tears of wheat, a turban of flowers

out of song and dance, beaded red silk

out of the throats of seven horses, stone eyes

out of the night, a dagger in the liver, a cord under the skin

out of the tail of sleep, the lucky tombs of children

out of the day's threadbare bag, dried dates

out of Allah's wool, a belt of beetle-*jnoun*

out of a knee—milk, almonds, diamonds, silver

out of the loom of the sun, the saffron heart of an oasis

At last, the sun's bag of horns, thorns, and horses
at last, words at the foot of a mother's silver tomb
at last, a tear dancing beautifully down a dry thread
at last, red wheat bleeding into the mouth of the heart
at last, a golden mirror helping praise a gazelle
at last, beetle eggs blackening the daggers of the moon
at last, stars arrowing the eyes of cockroaches and pigeons
at last, the luck of grass tents and leaf saddles
at last, rainwater on the head of a cat in the morning
at last, looms promising the sky to skin and knees
at last, wood dust and braids of indigo wool
at last, home handing a river the saffron night
at last, a bride with beaded hair salting a tail
at last, a life of riddles sleeping near a belt of fire
at last, shoes and turbans milking mountain almonds
at last, healing birds carpeting the henna oasis
at last, stones banging prayers into copper foxes
at last, a brother's sheep on Allah's amber sand
at last, triangles of *jnoun* livers and white diamonds
at last, bread in the face, meat in the throat of day
at last, an omen: a father hanging seven flowers
at last, silk, shells, and dung roaming out the door
at last, camels and goats greening the yellowed palms
at last, a year of dates, coins, and donkey cords
at last, a daughter's children singing and drumming in the trees

Yahya Frederickson is the author of *In a Homeland Not Far: New & Selected Poems* (Press 53, 2017), *The Gold Shop of Ba-'Ali* (Lost Horse Press, 2014), and four previous chapbooks: *The Birds of al-Merjeh Square: Poems from Syria* (Finishing Line Press, 2014), *Month of Honey, Month of Missiles* (Tigertail Productions, 2009), *Returning to Water* (Dacotah Territory Press, 2006), and *Trilogy* (Dacotah Territory Press, 1985, with Julie Taylor and Richard Schetnan).

His poems have appeared or are forthcoming in *Arts & Letters, Beloit Poetry Journal, Black Warrior Review, Cutthroat, Flyway, The Georgia Review, Hanging Loose, Michigan Quarterly Review, Mizna, New Moons: Contemporary Writing by North American Muslims, Ninth Letter, North Dakota Quarterly, Quarter After Eight, RHINO, The Southern Review, Verse Daily, WLA (War, Literature & the Arts), Witness,* and elsewhere.

His translations (with Muhammed Shoukany) of contemporary Saudi Arabian poetry appeared in *New Voices of Arabia: The Poetry: An Anthology* from Saudi Arabia (I.B. Tauris, 2012). His translations (with Gulzamira Mambetalieva) of contemporary Kyrgyz poetry have appeared in *World Literature Today.*

Yahya holds an MFA in Creative Writing from the University of Montana and a PhD in English from the University of North Dakota. Between graduate degrees he taught for six years in Yemen, initially as a Peace Corps Volunteer. He served as a Fulbright Scholar in Syria in 2005, Saudi Arabia in 2011, and Kyrgyzstan in 2016.

Yahya has been the recipient of two Academy of American Poets Thomas McGrath Memorial Awards, a Lake Region Arts Council/McKnight Foundation Fellowship grant, and residencies at The Anderson Center at Tower View, Grand Marais Art Colony, and Café Tissardmine (in Tissardmine, Morocco).

He teaches English at Minnesota State University Moorhead, on the occupied lands of the Dakota and the Anishinaabe.

www.ingramcontent.com/pod-product-compliance
Lightning Source LLC
Chambersburg PA
CBHW022102080426
42734CB00009B/1455